Open this book if you dare, a poet's lens into a world of the drowning, poems of the moment written with courage by a doctor. They express a dedicated healer's compassion and the limitations of caring and medicine.

What is it like to drown? What is it like to stand on shore, unable to swim, watching the foundering? Mary Dowd bears witness in these poems to what we can't change. She wrestles in language with the contradictions and the ironies that score our lives, as in the poem "Battered," which ends, "He was my best friend. / He was so good to me." And as she writes in "Feral"—

no doors on your heart,
no roof on your mind.

Nothing between you and the sky,
Nothing between you and the dirt,
Nothing between you and the knowledge
your final bed won't be much different.

Experience these poems like the doctor, like a lover, reading with hands to feel what it means when caught in life's riptides. Mary Dowd renders with a clear eye her own vulnerability and truth.

— Martin Steingesser, 2007-2009 Poet Laureate
of Portland, ME; author of three collections of poetry;
and a performance artist

Moving and refreshingly written from a perspective of someone who bears witness to lives overwhelmed by addiction. Verses will prove familiar to health care providers who are challenged by vocational dissonance: a fierce commitment to duty and deep compassion for people who are desperate for relief.

— Teresa DaVigo, PhD
Clinical Psychologist
Mental Health Service Area Manager
Kaiser Permanente Northwest

The desperation of trying to make a life when we've lost control. She sees the futility of trying to make sense of addiction. We notice her characters all around us, but we often turn away or don't really see. This unflinching portrait of real people says so much in few words and teaches us to really see. We're right there in the room with these people. Everyone has to figure it out for themselves. All we can do is be human, acknowledge, and accept.

— Michael Ware, MEd
Retired Health Education Specialist
for North Coast AIDS Project,
Humboldt County Public Health

If only at a distance we've all been touched by issues of addiction. As a doctor, Mary Dowd has allowed herself to come close. She has rubbed her hands up and down an addict's arms, feeling for veins. She has listened to the stories, to the hopes and despair, and has entered into all the complex contradictions of treatment. Out of this generosity, Dowd has created vivid and compelling portraits that honor the humanity of her patients. These beautiful and devastating poems touch the humanity of us all, reminding us that we each have a "carefully constructed self" and "self-appointed opinions." We too are in danger of being dead before we're happy. No easy answers here. As the poems make clear, whatever moral failings there are belong to us all as a society that has nodded out and escaped into our own forms of denial. Bless Mary Dowd for the work she does, and for the poems in *The Heroin Diaries* that are really about hope because they are poems of love, poems that give us back to each other, despite what addiction takes away.

— Betsy Sholl, 2006-2011 Poet Laureate of Maine,
Professor in the Master of Fine Arts Program in Writing
at the Vermont College of Fine Arts, and author
of eight collections of poetry

THE HEROIN
DIARIES

a book
of poems

LITTLE STORIES TO UNDERSTAND WHY

THE HEROIN DIARIES

a book of poems

LITTLE STORIES TO UNDERSTAND WHY

By Mary Dowd, MD

With photographs by
Joanne Arnold

The Permanente Press
Portland, Oregon • Oakland, California

About the cover image:
Sherri Ferrier, 44, homeless and battling a
heroin addiction, meets with Dr Mary Dowd
at Catholic Charities in Portland, ME, in 2015.
(Photo by Nikki Kahn/The Washington Post
via Getty Images).

© 2018 by The Permanente Press

Published 2018 by The Permanente Press
Portland, Oregon • Oakland, California

The Permanente Press is owned by The Permanente Federation, LLC
Oakland, California

THE HEROIN DIARIES

22 21 20 19 18   1 2 3 4 5

ISBN: 978-0-9770463-7-9
Library of Congress Control Number: 2018936109

Photographs by Joanne Arnold
Book design by Lynette Leisure
Printed in the United States of America

Dedicated
to the patients

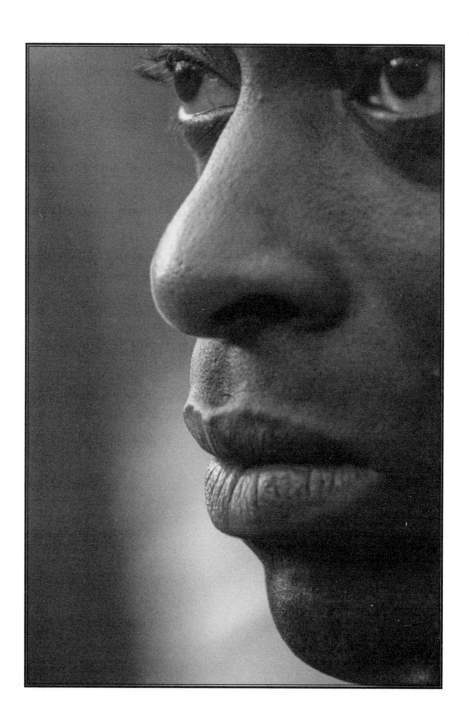

X

A Word about the Photographs:
Portraits of Men and Women in Recovery

Sometime last spring a friend told me about Joanne Arnold's work. My friend thought Joanne's images were a lot like my poems and told me go see her show in Portland, Maine. I went.

The photographs were a revelation. They were suggestive, haunting, and intimate. They didn't just tell about homelessness and addiction; they allowed the viewer to enter the story, to momentarily enter the lives of the subjects. They made me feel as if I'd arrived in the middle of things, in the middle of a thought, or at a moment of release, after the strife of a sleepless night, or just when something is about to happen. They reminded me of what James Joyce called "epiphanies." He used the term for moments of insight, which resulted from "a showing forth of character through simple actions, or details of appearance, and particular facts of their existence." Such details are always "showing forth" in these images. And the beauty in the details of the photos acts as a subtle force countering the disintegrating forces at work on the streets.

Yet, Joanne's work is never heavy with an agenda, intrusive, or exploitive, just clear-seeing and truthful, like Whitman's all-embracing vision; her art is a work of kindness and decency. The tone of her black-and-white photography magically expresses both the infinite hues and colors of night and the street while communicating the humanity and stature of the people who live in this usually unseen and unimagined world.

In working with Joanne to choose photos for the book, I wanted to focus on recovery as a counter balance to the weight of addiction, of what may seem in the poems an endless, hopeless struggle. The portraits we have chosen are of men and women in recovery. The images reveal their vulnerability and dignity, the distances traveled, damages sustained, and the grace, stamina and grit with which they greet every day. I am enormously grateful to Joanne and to her subjects for allowing me to include their portraits in this book.

Please note the placement of the photos in the book is random. None of the poems in the book are written about any of the individuals in the photos. In no instance does the poem preceding or following the photo have any connection to that person.

Contents

Definitions of Home

Contents

Foreword

*"Whatever inspiration is, it's born from
a continuous 'I don't know.'"*
— Wislawa Szymborska, Nobel Lecture, 1996

I have been staring addiction in the face for ten years now and I still don't know what it is. Late in life I took a job moonlighting at the county jail and found I had entered a world whose ground and spinning axis was addiction.

My early and middle years could be seen, on one level, as a one-way trajectory away from the chaos and heartache of growing up in an alcoholic household, in a town made up largely of first- and second-generation Irish immigrants who worshipped whiskey, the Pope, and President Kennedy, in no particular order. I did all the right things, got good grades, went to church and catechism, did not get pregnant, so I could go to college and live a responsible adult life. I thought I was following a rational course. But, the pulse propelling me, beating insistently beneath everything I did was, "Get me out of here, get me out of here."

So there I sat, in my mid-fifties, at the county jail, night after night, seeing one patient after another who was locked up because of something bizarre, brutal, unconscionable, or just plain stupid they had done while under the influence of drugs or alcohol, or in order to get money for more drugs and alcohol. It was relentless. It was chaotic, and it was heartbreaking. I was back in the world I had spent all my life running from. And I loved it.

I loved the patients. They were survivors, getting by somehow, without freedom, without choices. They were still full of life, full of imagination, full of plots and scams, able to laugh, despite, or maybe because of, the oppression and confinement.

And what I learned from them was how little I knew about addiction. They were in jail. They were detoxed. They had nothing but time, time to think about the choices they'd made, the serial disasters addiction had wrought in their lives. Yet they knew that despite their best intentions and their true heartfelt desire never to drink or use again, they were powerless not to. On the day of their release, even after months of sobriety, they would walk out of their cells, back to their old neighborhoods, back to their old friends, and back into the straitjacket of their old cravings and compulsions. Back to the world of dumb choices and desperate acts that would bring them right back to the county jail.

This fascinated me. How could something extraneous—a drug, a drink—how could it take over your will, despite your best efforts, against your better judgment, and run your life? How could a habit, a behavior, be so self-destructive, yet so compelling at the same time? It also felt like a spring thaw: some cold and stony place in my heart was opening, and I could begin to see a path through.

I have spent the last ten years learning all about addiction, reading books, going to conferences, teaching students, talking to the legislature and the public, and seeing patients. Ask me about the risk factors, the epidemiology, the treatment, the neurobiology, the genetics, the behaviors, and I can give you answers and sound like I know what I am talking about. But I am still in a continual state of "I don't know." I am still learning new things about addiction and life and the human heart every day from my patients.

These poems might give you the idea that treating addiction is a dismal business, that no one gets better, and things inevitably go from bad to worse. But this is not true. My patients, with good support from friends and family, and insurance that allows them access to treatment and counseling, transform their lives and thrive. But, it's the ones who don't have any of these advantages that touch me the most and inspire me to write about them.

It is not always easy doing this work. The patients can be tricky and challenging, at times, downright impossible. Their circumstances are often heartbreaking and hopeless. Several times a week I find myself in a quandary because what seems the best thing to do for a particular patient is at odds with what my medical training would dictate. And every day I find myself confronted with my own prejudices, my own rush to judgment, and my all too frequent failures of empathy or understanding.

These poems are born of a continuous "I don't know," of the many years I have spent pondering my patients and their disease. They are born of grief and the weight of sorrow these patients carry with them, their moments of despair and hopelessness in the relentless grip of their addiction, but also of their resilience and resourcefulness, and their remarkable ability to survive against enormous odds. They are born of my frustration that all I have to offer many of them, in the current political climate, in the face of a heroin epidemic, is fair-to-middling control of their withdrawal symptoms and a little kindness.

Keats defined something he called "negative capability, that is when a man is capable of being in uncertainties, mysteries, doubts, without any irritable reaching after fact and reason." I think of this at work when I'm confronted with a new patient problem and don't know what to do. It seems to be the right state of mind for a poet. But is it the right state of mind for a doctor?

Szymborska would say yes. "Whatever inspiration is, it's born from a continuous 'I don't know'." For her, those "whom inspiration visits … may include doctors, teachers, gardeners" or "a hundred more professions … whose work becomes one continuous adventure as long as they manage to keep discovering new challenges in it. Difficulties and setbacks never quell their curiosity. A swarm of new questions arises from every problem they solve."

I'd have to say, I don't know.

Author's Note

The details, descriptions, names, and
settings have been altered to protect patient
confidentiality. In the few poems where the
patient's identity may still be clear to their
acquaintances, I have received permission
from the patient to print the poem. In
some cases the patients have preferred
that I use their names. Some explanation
of terms used and notes on addiction
can be found at the end of the text.

Composite

He is 29, pale, and thin
almost skeletal.
He washes dishes, does day labor,
shovels snow, or hangs a sign.
He sleeps at the shelter
or in the park or in the woods.
He asks if he can weigh himself
to see how much he's lost this time.

She is 24,
full lips, green eyes, red-gold hair,
tall and slim and silent.
Her arms are covered like a sleeve tattoo,
in a swirling dance of scabs and scars
   and bruises.
Rust-brown puncture wounds
snake round and round.
Hard cords define each used up-vein.
Overall, the yellow green
of fading black and blues.
Underneath, pale white herringbone,
old slashes where she used to cut herself
when she was a kid.

Abused since she was 10,
her children, 2 and 4, and 8
live with her mother,
her grandmother,
or strangers.

He could be your son.
She could be your daughter.
You say, *Oh, no.*
Not her, not him,
not possible.
Not them.

He is 22, brown curly hair
broad shoulders, strong calves
a goalie's build.
Almost finished college,
but he got oxys for a twisted knee.
Now he's snorting heroin,
living on his best friend's couch
and selling some to get some more.

She is 19, blue eyes, blonde ponytail,
glitter on her hoodie.
She works weekends waiting table.
She's bought a car and wants to go to UMO,
but she keeps spending all her tips
on pills.

Now she's doing things
she really doesn't want to,
things she never thought she'd do,
just to get enough
to get her through the day,
enough so she can work
and not get sick.

He is your son.
She is your daughter.

What now?

Stigmata

So, where are you shooting?

Suppliant,
as if they are about to receive
a blessing or a burden,
something they must carry carefully
and not let drop,
they hold out both arms,
palms up,
for my inspection,
pale inner flesh
to the light.

Then they flip,
palms down,
weathered side up.
"Anywhere else?"
They roll up their pants to show me
tracks on their calves or ankles
or pull down their collar
to reveal a constellation, small red stars
along the jugular.

I run my hands along
the soft white under-belly of their arms,
rub my thumbs into the creases
at their elbows, probe the thin
translucent webs between fingers or toes,
press each fading black and blue,
each cord, each scab,
each puncture,
feeling for warmth,
fluid, swelling,
for something hot and angry
that wants to be let out.

Like Thomas sticking his fingers in the wounds,
mute, eyes wide, astonished to feel
the blood, still warm, the ragged flesh, the pain.

Like a blind man reading with my hands
a bitter tale of restless nights and desperate days,
the grim testament of their youth and age.

✦

Battered

Her face keeps collapsing into Tragedy's frown
eyes and mouth wrung and squeezed
like lemon rinds.

He was so good to me.
He gave me everything.
He knew everything about me,
and I knew everything about him.
He was my best friend,
my only friend.
He didn't like me to have other friends.

I wasn't doing nothin'.
I was cooking him an egg.
He took a lamp and smashed my face.
I'm the fourth,
the fourth he's mutilated,
that's what the cops said.
They said it's not the drugs.
It's just him.

He's got all my clothes,
all my stuff at his place
He paid for it.
It's just stuff.

He was my best friend.
He was so good to me.

Hansel

You know how you stand over the sink
to peel a carrot or a parsnip,
how you scrape off the outer
layer of dirt, then scrape a little more,
because you can, because
it's repetitive, like a mantra
and a bit fascinating how each flick
of your wrist is the same,
but each scraping comes out different,
some flat and thin, some round,
some oddly shaped, thick in the middle
and tapered on the ends
like knuckle-bones.

Each time I see Casey I think,
Someone's been peeling him,
scraping away the fullness in his cheeks,
paring the meat off his ribs and hips,
chiseling down the soft contours of his brow
and chin. His grin now stretches
ear to ear in his gaunt face, black holes
where his incisors used to be.

If I were a witch I could put him in a cage,
feed and fatten him, force Gretel to make
schnitzel and fork it through the bars.
He'd be safe and I'd come round once a week
to check his knucklebones.

I am only his doctor. I cannot stop him
ordering bathsalts from Canada,
klonopin from India, snorting Wellbutrin,
smoking crack, meth, spice
or shooting heroin into his neck veins.
All I can do is stop his vomiting
ease his cramps, drug him to sleep.
It won't be long now.

All I can do is repeat
the same pathetic suggestions,
get some help
go to counseling
go to AA, NA.

Useless as a trail of breadcrumbs.
✦

How a Man Becomes a Pencil

He must be tall, tall and thin,
so thin you could store water
in the hollows of his clavicles.
So thin his abdomen slopes down
like an alpine valley
from his Christ-on-the-cross ribs.
So thin his face can be remembered
only in profile.

He must be old, fifty, or so,
old enough to have survived
oceans of alcohol,
decades of catastrophe,
old enough to have spent
most of his youth,
and all of his adult life
(if you can call it that)
under the influence.

So that now he is in a permanent state
of catabolism
with beer, his only food,
whiskey, his only drink.

He must be yellow,
yellow hair, and his skin,
pale yellow, because his liver is imploding,
and leaving bilirubin backed up everywhere
and the whites of his eyes,
which are enormous now
in his scant face
are yellow too,
like fried blue eggs.

What is left of his mind
has narrowed to a thin sharp point
in which there are no
alternate presents, no
possible futures,
and the past, which may include
any love he once knew,
has been smudged into sentiment
or entirely erased.

And the sharp dark point of that pencil
moves in one direction only,
tracing a thin gray line
from one drink to the next.

And, if you follow that line
you will find him one day
crumpled in an alley
or face down in the bay.

✦

Jane

All angles,
a wisp, a twig,
a bundle of sticks,
legs crossed,
elbows out.

Back, again,
kicked out, again,
living at the shelter, again.

Two babies, one house
one college degree,
one disgusted husband,
why can't she stop?

If addiction is a disease of desire,
what is it she desires?

Should we ask if a degree in financial management,
an abacus life, riffling through other people's money,
will ever make anyone happy?
Should we explore the exemplary spouse,
pillar of the second Baptists,
brimming with tough love?

Should we question the limestone church
and green lawns, the good schools and good jobs,
the weekends at the shore and timeshares on the slopes?

Maybe she was meant to be
a hermit or a whore,
a sinner or a saint.
Now she's stuck,
stuck like a fly in amber,
like an egg in aspic,
stuck in the good life
in Camden, Maine.

And she can't even breathe.
✦

Kelly

Kelly's losing it,
the rounded edge
that keeps her in the foreground,
the third dimension
that stands her out against the sky.

The curve that draws us
to every human form,
the arc of limb or cheek,
the rounded weight of breast or hip,
that fits into the soft cup
of a human hand.

Heroin is planing it away.
Face and body flattened
to a geometric field,
diamonds, squares and triangles.
Paper-thin, she seems pasted
up against the wall where she leans
to have her breakfast smoke.

She's horizon to us now,
landscape,
graffiti painted on the bricks.

We don't see it.
We don't read it.
We just walk on by.

✦

Larry

Last time I saw Larry
he could barely keep his feet.
Even sober, he lunged
with every step toward
one wall or the other.

Now he's back,
detox number eighty-six,
twenty-five years of hepatitis C,
fifty years, with all his vital organs
floating in a bath
of Henny and Old Crow.

He raps on my door
like a woodpecker
and slides into the office
on the tails of a joke.

When I listen to his chest
he says,
I have the heart of a lion,
I'm a miracle,
a fucking miracle …

and a disaster.

Reading the Bones

When I see the frontal ridges jut
out from the hairline like rocky promontories
and the temples caved-in below, as if thumb-pressed,

When I see pupils, black as liquid coals
sunk in the bony bowl of dark orbits,
or shoulders rise like twin peaks
from the cratered lakes of deep clavicles,

When I note, as they walk toward me
how their whole being seems
to taper back from the midline
the way the head of a finely honed axe
recedes from the sharp edge of the blade,

Or how their faces, lips, limbs
seem dusted with white ash,
lusterless, bloodless, ghostly,

Then I know
heroin has become everything,
thirst and hunger, food and drink,
pulse and breath and bone,
reason for living,
reason enough for dying.

Then I know
this may be the last time,
the last time they make it back
to warmth, to light, a bed, a mat,
clean clothes, hot food.

Back to try one more time
for a place in rehab,
a room in a sober house,
a scholarship bed,
a miracle.

For a crack in the iron fist of the universe to open,
a chink, they can slip through,
almost unnoticed,
and survive.

✦

Addiction Medicine

In order to keep doing this I need a change of mind.

I need to set aside all notions, dearly held,
of progress, inner growth, development,
the faith that wisdom, hard won from experience,
can deliver us from folly.

In order to keep doing this I need a change of heart.

I need to pull the plug on my comic puffed-up valentine,
let hope leak out like helium,
unhook the chambers each from each
and let the chaos in.

In order to keep doing this I need a change of scene.

I need to wrench my eyes from their all too sordid pasts,
full of misery and mayhem, and keep my gaze
from wandering to their all too certain futures,
predictable as pain.

I need to fix my focus firmly in the present

To see them as they are just now, brimming with hope
and earnest purpose. Now, at this point of insight,
this moment of good will. Because it's all we have,
all we ever have,

All that really matters.

Amy Says

She used it all,
the whole fucking lot of it.
They stashed it in her car
to keep it safe.

Half a kilo of heroin,
twenty grams of coke.
Now it's gone.
It's fucking gone,
up her nose
and down her veins.

Now they're parked in the woods
outside her parents' house.
Now they're waiting by the playground
where her son goes to school,
and the sheriff's got a deputy
sitting in his class.

✦

Johnny

The last time I saw Johnny we stood by the coffee stand
at the soup kitchen talking.

His face tanned and scored from decades in the weather,
his leather jacket fitted from wide shoulders
to slim waist, hair and mustache long
but neat, looking a little rakish
with a bright plaid scarf
tucked into his lapels.

We talked of getting older, the long winter,
the usual chat of strangers,
his gestures wide, his consonants,
a little furry. I could tell he liked me
standing there, talking to him.

I thought of him this week,
wondered why I never see him
at detox or the ER.

Today he came in early, an hour before lunch,
blue parka streaked with dirt,
too big for him, too heavy for the season.
Gotta piss, gotta piss, can't wait, can't wait.
Stooped and shuffling, hair caked and snarled,
arms hanging out in front,
simian, like a chimp.

Two years and all his polish gone,
his natty charm, his fetching smile,
his kind blue eyes.

His little light gone out,
only darkness left.

✦

Liam the Wanderer

Moves from state to state to regulate his habit.

He's got a point. We always say:
move out of that neighborhood,
ditch your friends, delete your contacts.

Liam's got it down, three days, tops,
he's gone. No time to learn the ropes,
no time to imprint places, names or faces.

Three days, he's in a freight car
heading west to harvest sugarbeets
in Minnesota or lettuce in Salinas.

Two weeks, two grand,
then gone again, fighting wildfires
in Texas or Montana.

Two grand! You'll blow it all,
You'll never get out west.
Stay here, get some clean time,
get some help.

Heroin addicts, you know,
they don't live that long.

He says,
I've accepted that.

Next Thing You Know

Bill's at the mall,
selling bird houses,
to raise some dough
for his halfway house.
Getting late, time to go.

Next thing you know
he's gone to Applebee's
to take a leak.
There's his dealer
waiting for a seat.

Next thing you know
he's bought 10 grams.
House money's gone,
slips out the back,
he'd better scram.

Next thing you know
he's shot it all.
Five grams a day
won't get him where
he wants to go.

Next thing you know
he's on the floor, pale
and blue, barely breathing.
Red lights flashing,
sirens blaring.

Next thing you know
he's waking up
in a hospital gown
sweating, shaking, puking,
wondering how it all went down.

✦

Sometimes

He says he only tries it when he's drunk,
or high, or in a blackout.
It's not an option when he's sober.

She says the same, how she woke once
to find a rope in her hands, perfectly knotted
and thick enough to hold her weight.

And the self, where does the self go?

It seeks some huddled cavern underground
whose hollow walls will magnify its sound
and call and calls.

It watches, wide-eyed, as the black tide rolls
swiftly in to cover it in silence
and stands on tiptoe,

Nose tilted up to breathe the final inch
of air and prays, prays for the tide to turn,
which it does

Sometimes.

Saturday on the 7th Circle

Louisa, 62, lies adrift
on the wide white sea of her bed,
curled sideways,
swaddled in johnnies.
It could be a bundle of rags
but for the small tremors
that shudder through it.

Eyes tightly closed,
lips pressed to a thin line,
she will not talk or move.
She will not take her meds.
She will not say she has a plan,
a cache of pills, a knife, a rope.
She will not eat or bathe or dress.
She will only say she can't go on.
She will not say no or yes.

Sam, 49, sits on the edge
of his unmade bed
in his darkened room,
hands sinking through his knees,
head sinking to his chest.
On his way to hang himself
when a friend found him
and brought him in.

He is angry, angry at himself,
so angry it fills the room,
sucking out all the oxygen.
It is unbearable, almost unbreathable,
to sit and look and listen.
He has destroyed everything,
his work, his wife, his home, his family.
He has nowhere to go but down,
down to dangle
at the end of a rope.

Jamaica, 21,
seems to be wearing nothing at all
under her hospital sheets this morning.
She flounces from side to side.
When I tell her she has Hepatitis C
she flips her back to me
covers her head with her pillow
and shouts,

I might as well kill myself!
Who's gonna wanna go out with me now?

But Jamaica,
full of attitude and flourish
is safe.

The other two need time,
two days, maybe three, to resurrect,
for hope, which has been crucified,
to rise again.

Fifth Business

Phonecall from N, contrite, subdued,
so soft spoken I can barely hear him,
calls to say he's out of town,
can't come in for a refill.

Last week, stoned, weaving through traffic,
smudging his sandwich into his mouth,
swaying like a cobra on my exam table.
I hauled him up and out
before he crashed.
Back on his feet,
FUCK THIS!
and out he slammed.

Now I tell him there's pot in his urine again,
I can't refill him,
and feel his spirits drop an octave.

If only you could just work with me.
I've got a script for medical marijuana.
My HIV meds make me sick,
throwing up sick.
Weed helps, it does,
really, it does.

I can't say I don't doubt it's true,
because I do,
doubt it's true, but …
it could be true.

I tell him, *I'm sorry, I can't work with that.*
Not with him, in the game,
running the streets, crooked for so long
never even knew straight.

I give him names of other docs, other clinics
where he could maybe sell the weed deal,
maybe.

And as we talk
I feel the gyre of his life
reverse itself,
from winding up out of heroin
HIV, homelessness,
to spiral back down
into a vortex of obsession,
overdose and death.

I see myself too,
where I don't want to be,
at the turning,
a bit player,
just a walk on,
minor, but crucial
in the opera of this life.

Escape Artist

Phil comes in to say he's at it again,
clean for a few months, now a bottle every night,
started slowly, doesn't know when,
doesn't know how,
doesn't know why.

Have you gone to any meetings?
I don't like groups.
Are you alone every night?
Mostly.

(Has she finally had enough,
is she plotting *her* escape
and you don't even know it?)

Have you read the books I gave you?
I only read fiction.
I need to escape.

The irony escapes him.

If this were a play
I could say something grandiloquent,
full of melancholy wisdom,
something that sounds profound,
but probably isn't.

Your drinking is the mother of all escapes
a side-door out of life, a series of little deaths,
trial runs at oblivion.
Easier by far than waking up
to the beauty and the terror all around you.
Easier by far than claiming your abject weakness
and your shining courage.

You have a problem reason and will cannot solve.
Consider paradox, renunciation,
the meaning of surrender.

Consider surrendering your carefully
  constructed self,
your self-appointed opinions
of who you are, what you do,
and what this life should be.
You need to do what you don't like to do
or you'll be dead before you're happy.

The universe, the stars themselves
are knocking on his cranium,
using alcohol to shake him down
and wake him up,
to tell him something's gone awry,
terribly awry.

But, there he sits,
square brow, square jaw,
square shoulders,
stuck in the box of himself
and no way out.

Dr. Jekyll

What were you doing with all that suboxone,
one script from me and one from Dr. X?

He's not going to tell me he's selling it,
but I'm feeling ill-used.
I just want to rant.

So, he starts and goes on and on
with many open-handed gestures
to underline his innocence.
He wasn't sure of his options,
he wanted to keep them open,
he didn't know what was going to happen,
here, there or anywhere, really.
Would he stay at this clinic, would he go to
    another?
And it was only for a few weeks.

November to April?
Well, he was taking it,
he needed a little extra in the afternoon.
Double your dose?

Finally, he realizes, it's over,
our tortured relationship.
I'm not going to keep treating him
or even taper him.

It starts again,
the gestures,
the explanations,
the talk goes on and on.
Then he starts to cry,
says how sick he'll be
tonight, tomorrow,
then back out on the streets scoring heroin,

AND THEN I'LL BE DEAD!

And I know it's true,
not today or next week,
but sometime, sometime soon.
Next month, next year,
five years from now,
he'll be found in a room not fit for vermin
with a needle in his arm, and I complicit
in his sordid end.

Now he's getting hysterical.
It's starting, he says.
The cramping, the anxiety,
he can feel it,
the churning in his gut,
the aching in his calves,
he's starting to withdraw right now!

I look at him and see a soul in hell
and tell myself to have compassion for
    his suffering.
Oh, not to take him back, or give him
    what he wants,
just to feel his pain,
but fail.

I have had my revenge.
I have seen him pinned and wriggling.

Implacable,
I walk out.

Darkness Visible

Nathan seems distilled,
refined down to a small spirituous essence,
like drops coalesced at the bottom
of a clouded alembic.

His yellow irises, framed
with long black lashes, cat's eyes,
follow me as I move about
examining lungs and heart,
ears and mouth. He sits quite still,
as if a touch could crumble him,
the way an ancient snakeskin
found in a desert cave
seems perfectly intact until,
at a breath, it shatters to dust
and drifts away.

When I ask where he is shooting
he thrusts out his fists, curled
palms up, unfurls his fingers,
one by one to show me the purple-
red hash of his fingertips, then removes
his socks, to reveal his toes, the same.

It is as if the small kernel of night
that lay sleeping inside him
has split open, and from it shadows
have grown and spread and filled
the poor vessel of his body
eating him like maggots
from the inside out.

And now the shadows have reached
the perimeter, his fingertips and toes,
and will emerge
to eat the air around him,
until nothing is left,
not even a dry husk,

Then move on, insatiable,
to the next warm body.
✦

Relapse

Perhaps you could think of yourself as a simple organism,
a fruit fly, say, or a protozoa.
Make it simple, but make it a mosaic.
Give it two distinct genotypes.
Dedicate one to life and one to death.

Perhaps you thought of death as a terminal event:
bucket kicked, dust bitten, farm bought.
But, you'd be wrong.

Fact is, you are both living and dying
at the same time.
Your cells endlessly blooming
and wilting, sloughing and scattering,
the old dissolving to make room for the new.

And the urge to move forward
is always at odds with the urge to stop,
dead in your tracks, pull the covers up
over your head and sleep forever.

So, think of yourself, this simple organism,
with one line of cells that gropes
toward the light and one line that festers,
in love with the dark.

And you must somehow balance
the yes and the no, the yin and the yang,
the light and the dark of it.

Each time you sink into fuck it,
poor me, why bother, who cares,
the dark gains, the light loses.

Each time the fog in your mind
curls its tendrils tighter around
your memory, your judgment, your will.

Each time your body shrivels,
your heart falters, your spirit shrinks.
Your small ration of hope, purpose, and meaning dwindles.
Each time there is less light left to push back the night.
✦

Feral

Their faces are thick and red,
coarsened by drink and weather,
their eyes, wide and wary.
Their hands are rough-cut boards,
their feet unmentionable.
Walls and windows hem them in,
chairs and beds don't fit.
Even sober,
they can't live in a house.

Even in winter
they come to the shelter
only on the coldest nights.
Once inside, they start to pace.
They prefer a blue tarp
in the woods,
a sleeping bag
stuffed with newspapers.

It's the proximity
they can't abide,
so they keep a steady level
of whiskey in their blood
to keep from lashing out
like tomcats over territory,
over insults misperceived,
over voices saying things
only they can hear.

Whiskey blunts the edge,
the edge of exposure,
the feeling every day
that comes from having
no doors on your heart,
no roof on your mind.

Nothing between you and the sky.
Nothing between you and the dirt.
Nothing between you and the
    knowledge
your final bed won't be much different.
✦

Definitions of Home

Acute angle
where two brickfaces
abut under a metal stair,
that sections the wind and sun
into manageable portions.

Cardboard box
stuffed with newspapers
positioned just right
to catch the heat
above a sidewalk grate.

High curbstone
where you can sit
with legs bent or stretched,
where you can fall over
without significant injury.

Blue tarp by the tracks,
pan, towel, knife,
can opener,
hat, parka, gloves,
extensive outdoor plumbing.

Backpack holding
one shirt, four sox,
two boots, one bottle,
forty ounces high gravity,
six quarters.

Metal shopping cart
diverted from Hannaford's
stuffed with three black trashbags,
two, empties,
one, clothes.

Ninety-seven Toyota,
food and clothes in trunk.
At bedtime
kids curl up in front,
you stretch out in back.

Or, maybe,
it's just a patch of linoleum,
four gray tiles
by the nurses' station,
where you can stand

For a chat, for a joke,
with people who know your name,
know you've cut your hair,
or shaved your beard,
or found new shoes.

Where you can stand
for a minute,
maybe two,
under cool fluorescent light
and feel the sun.

Luck

When did you have your first drink?
Well, m' first drunk was at nine.
'Fore that, m' father usta put beer in m' bottle.
I was colicky, he'ped me sleep.

When he opens his mouth to say, 'ah,'
two sinister black spikes,
all the teeth he's got,
rise from his bottom gum
like the gates of Mordor.

But they don't bother him, never have.

Says he lives by luck.
Can't work no more,
takes whatever comes his way,
what people give him,
or collecting bottles.
Sometimes he finds money on the ground.

He's lucky that way.
✦

Grace on the Corner of Oxford and Preble

Sometimes you can see it descending
like that upside-down dove.

Eddy swirls into the clinic like a leaf in a high wind.
Starts in with his ready line of patter.

New baby, angry girlfriend, rent to pay,
job offers, cleaning, painting, raking.
If you could just give me a script
Just to get me through
I'll come back on Monday and do a urine.
I swear I will.
It'll be clean.
I swear it.

Not even twenty-two,
the world already heavy on his shoulders.
No urine, no script,
see his counselor,
come back Monday.

Deflated, he leaves,
stands on the corner,
thumbs hitched in his jeans,
cap backwards,
surveying the scene,
hungry, craving,
wanting, weighing.

But at this moment,
no faces he knows,
no deals going down.
He slumps.
His gaze hits the distance.

He straightens and walks on.
✦

Angels in Old Age

They come to detox still dressed in leather,
vests or jackets, faded jeans with stringy knees.
They still wear their pirate kerchiefs
low across their brows and knotted at the nape.
Their moustaches and sideburns, bushy still,
are white now, their ponytails thin wisps of gray.

They've had a thousand wrecks, a thousand brawls,
a thousand surgeries to glue them back together.
They list to port or starboard and sometimes sport
a plastic eye or wooden leg.
Their spinal discs, ground to dust
by the vibrations of the road,
their noses, broken and rebroken,
spread out across their cheeks,
a curious topography.
Beneath their skin skulls and dragons
weep blue charcoal tears.

Because now it's gone, the freedom
of the road, the wild wind in their faces
and the women, long of limb and hair,
wrapped like snakes around them.

Now there's nothing left,
nothing but backache, whiskey and the stories,
half-remembered, half-invented,
stories even they are sick of telling,
sick of hearing.

✦

Ballad

Nicki's working the nightshift
trying not to drink.
Working midnight to seven
gives you time to think.

She thinks about her kids.
The state took them away.
She thinks they're better off.
They'd just be in her way.

She thinks about her honey
locked up in the jail.
She thinks she's better off
if she don't pay his bail.

Glad he's in the tank,
he'd spend her pay on booze.
She's got stuff in storage
she doesn't want to lose.

If she leaves him till court
she'll end up black and blue.
Damned if you don't
and damned if you do.

She's tired, tired, tired,
more than she can say.
But she'll work any hours,
she's got fines to pay.

Wonders where she'll sleep,
her shift ends in a few,
wonders every night,
ain't nothing new.

Kicked out of the shelter
for getting in a fight.
The other girl started it.
It just ain't right.

She can't go Franny's.
Last time she was there
she took half her xannies,
she just wanted to sleep.

She can't go to Harry's.
He won't keep it in his pants.
She's bone weary and hungry,
no mood for romance.

She can't go to Louie's,
though he always makes her laugh.
He's got scabies, lice and bedbugs
and never takes a bath.

Seven a.m., sun comin' up,
she heads to Dunkin's
for a donut and a cup
with two milk and two sugars

To keep her on her feet
till she can get to the park;
if the cops let her be,
she'll finally get some sleep.
✦

Tares

I see them in the street,
the ones who didn't make it,
the ones who couldn't hack it,
not even for a week or two,
not even for a day,
staying sober.

They wanted it, but not enough,
or thought that it was something else,
such as peace, heart's ease,
happiness.
The same things
they were seeking to begin with,
but found, to their dismay,
that it was sickness first,
then pain,
then endless struggle
and always and everywhere,
anxiety.

I see them lounging in the library,
wandering down Oxford Street,
or hurrying up Congress,
intent and purposeful.

It's the future, not the past
that trails them through the streets
and haunts their idle hours.
It casts an eerie glow,
an aura of chaos,
a frisson of futility.

Something in the air around them,
something in the energy exhaled,
something to do with being doomed.
✦

Back

Twenty-two,
fourth overdose,
narcan'd five times
before they got him to the E.R.
They kept him overnight.
His chest still hurts
from the CPR.

He knows how lucky he is,
lucky to be back,
to be upright, sensible
of the pain in his ribs,
the ache in his legs, the sweats and chills,
happy to get a bed in detox.
He knows he has to stop.

Safe now,
for five days,
maybe seven.

Then what?

No insurance, no money,
no medicine, no rehab.

Then nothing.

Back to the streets,
back to the shelter,
back to his dealer,
back to the shadowlands.

A Mere Anatomy

... A mere anatomy ... — William Shakespeare, The Comedy of Errors

Each time I see Richard now
he wanes a little more
into his concavity.

His back, curved
base to skull,
describes a perfect C.

His belly, scaphoid,
hugs his spine.
His face, withered walnut,

Repeats the curve,
nutcracker nose
to wiry red goatee.

Month to month,
week by week,
his crescent shrinks

Thinner, paler, dimmer
till all that's left,
a mere cuticle of light

That blazes still,
compressed
to its pure essence:

Fury, at himself,
the booze,
the world.

◆

Odyssey

First some panhandling
  and petty thievery,
    then four 40s and a fifth.

Climb the embankment,
  slide and slip,
    up to the overpass

by St John's Street
  to end it all.
    Out he jumps,

And down he rolls,
  loose limbed from whiskey,
    scarce a scratch.

Three more 40s,
  pass out in the snow
    piled high behind Whole Foods.

Sirens wailing, EMTs,
  lines and hotpacks
    to his groin and chest,

IVs, O2, intubate,
  BAL of 6.2,
    then a bed in ICU.

Transfer to psych,
  a holding pen,
    until he's safe

To be let loose again.
  Discharged, homeless,
    hopeless, clueless.

Two more 40s and a fifth
  If only I could drink enough
    to not wake up.

Police escort,
  back to ED,
    back to psych,

Holding pen,
  until he's safe
    to be let loose again.

And the nights
  so cold now
    and the days so short.

✦

Benny

Benny's face looks stepped on,
the outer edges slowly sinking
in around his nose,
the way dough, punched down, caves
to the center.

Forty years treading water
in ocean of vodka.
Twenty-five years of HIV.
Roofless, jobless,
cashless, wifeless
for twice that long.
Half a century and he's still here.

God's got a plan for me.

Curious plan, I say.

Whatever it is,
He better tell it to me soon.
✦

World Records

A gallon a day,
Smirnoff's.
All by yourself?
Mostly.

Eight 40s.
High Gravity?
Yep.

15 Natty Daddys.
Ninety-nine cents each.

300 Corricidin.
Why?
It's like Dex.

100 Ambien
Milligrams?
No, pills. I can't sleep.
Where do you get it?
Fedex from India.

225 mg Valium
plus 450 mg oxycodone.
Walking, talking, making sense.

Heroin?
14 grams a day.
IV?!!!
No, I snort it.
If I boot it, I only need 7.
✦

Jake

It's the second time he's bagged it,
missed the day. The day
he was supposed to come to clinic,
stand at the toilet and urinate
with an audience of one, to verify
that the pee was inside his bladder
before it was inside the cup.

Now he goes on about his ADD,
he never can remember things,
never keep the days straight.
Anyway, there's a warrant out,
he's gotta lie low.

Last week it was cocaine.
Ran into a friend, it was there,
it was free, no excuses,
but really, what else could he do?

I tell him I have to taper him.

FUCK THAT!
I DON'T BELIEVE IT
I DON'T FUCKING BELIEVE IT!
YOU'RE OUT TO GET ME
I KNOW YOU ARE
YOU DON'T WANT ME TO GET CLEAN.

He's right of course.
I think he's selling half of what I give him.
He storms out,
GO FUCK YOURSELF!

Jesus, wouldn't I love to,
duck into the staff bathroom
and emerge moments later
tousled, pink-cheeked, starry-eyed.

Wouldn't it be heaven
if we could just go fuck ourselves,
bypass all the heartache and anxiety
that sex with a partner entails,

The tweaking and soothing of egos,
the crossed signals, missed chances,
the bottomless pit
of self-doubt and inadequacy.

If we could all just masturbate,
or watch internet porn,
or find meaning and connection
with an inflatable doll.

I know people do,
but I mean the rest of us,
the vast middle of the curve
between sociopath and saint.

Like a priest dispensing blessings,
he winds slowly through the waiting room
stopping at each client,
FUCK YOU AND YOU AND YOU
and then he's gone.

This is Just to Say

If you keep shooting heroin
into your jugular
you will not live to see forty.
You know it, I know it.
Forgive me for stating the obvious.
It's all I can do.

Trust

Now, that I have to keep a needle's eye
for the shifty gaze,
perfect pitch for the glib excuse,
the story that goes on
too long: the bus that didn't come,
the grandmother who died so suddenly,
then died again, and one last time,
the boyfriend who hid their clothes
or put valium in their coffee.

I say I don't mind being scammed.
All part of the disease,
a way of life, really,
survival skill, etc., etc.
Unless absolutely necessary,
I don't confront them.
Why bother, only to get more of the same.

Protestations of innocence: *I know my credibility is pretty low right now.*
Puzzled considerations: *There must be a problem at the lab.*
Or sheer bewilderment: *Someone must have put that cocaine in my urine.*

I, myself, am indifferent honest,
willing to arrange most facts to further
my own comfort or opinions.
Why fault them for doing the same?

Trust,
I used to say trust.
The doctor-patient relationship is based on trust.
If you don't like Dr. So-and-so,
here's your records, what's your hurry.

Now I see it's something else entirely.
Something I am learning and forgetting every day.
Something deeper than trust,
larger than empathy,
more useful than understanding.

Acceptance.
Acceptance of who they are right now
and belief unspoken
in who they could become.

Addiction

I

Sometimes I see a mother large,
white and pillowy, calling,
calling her children home,
night coming on,
the wind sharpening its teeth.
She calls and they come.

She lies on her side like a sow
and spreads her fat pink thighs.
They stuff down their horror and disgust
and dive headfirst back into the watery void
to drift for a while without fear or
   connection,
to know only this floating world,
this warm, soft absence.

II

Sometimes, I see a friend, a best friend,
someone to feed you flattery and fiction.
Someone to tell you, yes,
you're right, you're always right
and you have suffered pain
and loss and misunderstanding,
the worst since time began,
and you deserve a break, a rest,
a ticket out of here.
Someone to pry the nails out of your
   hands and feet
and give you this cool tomb to lie in.

III

Sometimes, I see the evil twin,
the twisted sister,
the one so hungry, needy,
empty and alone,
nothing will ever fill
the blackhole in her heart.

IV

Sometimes, I see trickster,
coyote, so cool, so in the know.
He takes your money
and leaves you low,

but keeps you on a string.
Each time you strike it rich,
fresh off the fishing boat,
pockets stuffed with cash,
he reels you in.

V

Sometimes, I see a dragon,
an enormous dragon
from a Chinatown parade,
a hundred arms and legs,
giant head and eyes
swaying side to side,
roaming the streets,

Stalking the strong,
the musclemen,
brash and hip,
always proving something
to somebody on a street corner.

Preying on the weak,
lost in grief, self-hatred or despair,
all out of chances,
crumpled on a curb.

Devouring the children,
young or old, children born of children,
abandoned and abused,
consuming their bodies, hearts and minds
and wanting more, always wanting more,
and always getting what it wants.

VI

Always, I see a simple soul, half-formed
like a fetus, spinning like a top,
caught in a barbed coil of desire and deceit.
Spinning, spinning, always spinning,
not knowing how to stop,
not knowing even if it wants to,
and terrified of trying.

Message in a Bottle

"Drink me," says the note tied to its neck.
Drink me and grow tall, like Alice.
So tall, your head will scrape the ceiling,
your Popeye arms will pop out
at the window and the door.

So tall, you will strut the streets
in seven-league boots,
cruising for a bruising,
till your face becomes a spin-art palette,
red and black and purple
and your nose a crooked trail.

"Drink me," it says and grow small,
like Alice. So small, no one will see
you creep along the wall and dart
into the nearest hole.
No one will hear your voice,
a little squeak, when you have to speak
your mind, your heart, your pain.

"Drink me," it says and expand.
Feel your spirit blossom with warmth,
good will, a friend to all mankind.
Watch your belly broaden, first with fat,
then with fluid. Fat, sleek and slippery
like a seal to slide right off the rocky coast
of work and wife and worry
into a wine-dark sea.

"Drink me," it says and shrink
to a cocklebur with a hundred
sticky points to catch and keep
each injury and insult
and never let them go.

Drink me and grow blank,
be numbed. Forget the backache,
the toothache, the heartache,
the death, the divorce,
the accident, the rape,
the fucked-up parents who shot you up
to calm you down
when you were twelve years old,
the step-father who killed your dog.

Drink me, and disappear.
Slip like loose change into the dark
    gritty space
between the cushions on the couch,
into the gray smoky hole beneath the
    sidewalk grate.

Lie insensate in the cave beyond dreams
where death, feeling your warmth,
stirs in his sleep and snuggles
each time a little closer.

Drink me, it says,
drink me, drink me, drink me,
again and again and again.

Drink me and extinguish.

Poster Child

Ed calls himself the poster child,
says he's done it all, done it right, too.
Been to Plymouth House, St Francis',
Serenity, Our Father's.
Been there, done that,
got a hundred t-shirts.

Big handsome guy, raven hair, amber eyes,
says it's different now. He and his buds
used to drive down to Lowell,
pick up a few grams, take their share,
sell a few, make a little dough,
drive down again the next day.

Used to be in and out,
in and out of the life,
use a little, catch a habit, detox.
Stay clean for a few,
get a job, get some money,
start again. In and out.

Now it comes from far away.
Now it's got claws instead of hooks.
Now they're killing people over turf.
Now he can't stop when he wants to,
and he gets so much sicker every time.

His ex says he can't stop
because he doesn't care,
doesn't care enough
about using, about not using,
about anything.

What will you do after you leave here?

Try not to die.
✦

Lacrimae Rerum

Dan has five
blue tears
tattooed down his cheek.

Last year, sober
almost six months,
his first winter out of jail.

Thanksgiving, he cooked
two big turkeys
for his sober house.

He graduated,
got some furniture,
a TV, a CD player,

Some pads and pencils
for drawing, a journal
to write in, a desk.

But his kids didn't like it.
They kept bringing him weed,
then a little vodka,

Then a few oxys.
By February
he was back inside.

✦

The Suit

A size too big, padded shoulders
off kilter, trousers rolled once
like a cuff, but not a cuff,
white shirt, red tie.

He sits in a row of plastic chairs
lined up outside my office,
like a kid waiting for a birthday party
in his brother's clothes.

Sunday in detox, same suit,
face down on the bed,
rumpled, snoring, wingtips
hanging off the edge.

Court on Monday.
Clinic on Tuesday.
Same suit, chin shaved,
hair slicked. So earnest

About wanting to get clean
do a good program
go to school, get a good job
and so lost,

Lost in his clothes.
✦

The Queen of Sorry

Ruth calls herself
the queen of sorry.
Sorry, she can't come in
she's not feeling up to par.
Sorry, but she won't go out,
she can't get in the car.

Sorry, but those dishes
from yesterday
or the day before
are staying in the sink
and the laundry,
on the floor.

Sorry, but, she can't seem
to change her sweats
or wash her hair.
Sorry, a shower's
just not in the cards
and, really, who could care?

Yes, she's been to counseling.
Been to AA, been to NA,
been to group,
knows the triggers,
knows the slogans,
knows the scoop.

Sorry, but these pills don't work.
Neither did the last ones,
or the ones the time before.
As of now, she's done, *finis*!
She doesn't see the point of
talking, talking, talking anymore.
✦

Shoes

It's alcohol, really.
That's my problem,
not the dope.

But you just OD'd on heroin.

Only because I hadn't used lately.
Lost my tolerance.

You still OD'd,
even though you knew that.

I guess.

Anything else I can help you with?

Shoes.

Shoes?

I got no shoes.
I was out.
The medics came and took me.
They forgot my shoes.

✦

St. Liam

Like light
  poured from a
    Vermeer window,

October sun
  spills west to east,
    flames grass,

Dazzles chrome,
  the stop and go of cars
    along the median.

GOING SOUTH
  NEED CASH FOR FOOD
    PLEASE GIVE

Liam works the strip,
  cadging ones and dimes
    and quarters.

The sinking sun
  glints his stubble
    red to gold,

Leaves his Goth tattoos
  and metal studs
    in shadow.

His army coat,
  soft in the sun,
    glows mossy green.

Liam on his way
  from Maine
    to New Orleans,

Cast out by family,
  scorned friends,
    beset by demons

Of his own devise.
  A rocky path
    through desert places

With loneliness
  before, behind
    and all around.

Liam on his pilgrimage,
  half in shadow,
    half in light,

Enhaloed at this moment,
  electric
    green and gold.

✦

Weekend on Call

Yesterday, I was Mother Theresa.
Get up, get dressed, you have to go.
I don't have nowhere to go.
It was raining.
It was November.
I let him stay.

Today I am cost-effective,
a discharging machine,
toeing the hospital's bottom line:
money, money, money.
Get up, get dressed, you have to go.
It is still November.
It is still raining.
I don't have nowhere to go.

Thanks to the fierce cunning of discharge planners,
the pathological goodness of caseworkers
and sheer dumb luck,
he has been housed a dozen times this year:
a bed in a therapeutic community,
a room in a sober house,
a halfway house, a bridge program,
a re-entry house, a rooming house,
even his own apartment,
only to abandon each
for whiskey and the streets.

Get up, get dressed, you have to go.

I don't have nowhere to go.

The Other Side

Bruce almost skips into the exam room,
high spirits, full of it,
says something crazy
about me being *the luvvv doctor*
and tells me he's been spending a lot of time
on the other side.

Left detox 3 days ago,
shot his usual, quarter gram is all,
and went out.
Narcan'd four times
before they got him back.

Dead serious about wanting to quit
and dead takes on a whole new meaning.

No home.
No family.
No insurance.
No dice.
A line on a waiting list,
his name on a grubby yellow pad
is all he gets.

Eyes Wide Shut

She closes her eyes when I talk
and opens them when she talks.

I wanted to be off opiates BEFORE I delivered!
I don't want my baby on drugs.
I left St Mary's because I didn't want treatment.
Now you're telling me the same thing.
Fuck!

She's spent seven months, sick most of it,
withdrawing, baby jonesing too,
weaning herself down to 2 mg
every other day.

Now she hears again, eyes closed,
from another stupid, boring doctor,
who may as well be from Mars,
for all she knows about what her life is like,
it was futile, worse than futile.
Harmful.

She says she'll think about it,
opens her eyes and walks out.

Blind

I

The river fluke is carried in the spit of the black fly.
When she bites she leaves her larva underneath your skin.
The larva grow to worms, mate, multiply, then set up house.
But they need a certain mass, different in each case,
before they renovate your skin from itchy, bumpy, spotty
to paper thin and scaly, then spread out to colonize
your organs and your eyes.

A few bites here and there, you're still ok.
Comes the tipping point, the worms have taken over
and you're blind.

II

One drink here and there, a few with friends on Friday night,
you're still ok. A few too many on the weekend,
then every weekend, then two or three to kick back
after work and watch the tube. Then a 6-pack every night,
and one at noon on Saturday to ease you through the chores.
Then one to cure the Monday morning headache
and steady up your nerves.

Comes the tipping point, the worm has taken over
and you're blind.

III

You stare into the mirror, but you don't see
your coarse red skin, your drooling liquid eyes,
the way your jaw hangs slack and loose,
your expression vague and stupid, like a trout.

You don't see the black craters of despair
beneath the sparks of anger in your lover's eyes.
You don't feel your children flinch from your embrace,
or see their faces turn to stone each time you bend to kiss them.

They speak but you don't hear
the bitterness, frustration and disgust,
or worse, the weary resignation
when you act just as expected.

Life proceeds
from the wrong end of the telescope,
far-away and indistinct
through the ice-cold scrim
of your total self-absorption.

The worm has taken over and you're blind.
You're blind, and deaf and dumb,
and you don't even know it.
You buy another fifth
and turn it off, all off,
like the remote.

✦

Circling Sanity

Sniffing the perimeter,
nosing out the coffee, the traffic,
the nine to five,
not coming too close,
not sure if it's a good smell
or a bad one.

Come in,
make an appointment.
Maybe you keep it.
Maybe you don't.
Too high, too hungover, too anxious.
Make another.
Get on meds.
Get a job,
Wendy's, McDonald's, Dunkin's.
Get paid.

Call to say
your ride didn't show,
the bus was late,
your uncle died.
Make another appointment,
another and another,
don't show.

One day you look up,
you're thirty-eight or forty.
You've been asleep,
checked into Neverland,
ten years, twenty,
a long time gone.

Your children, scattered,
tossed like dice to family,
friends or foster care.
You sleep on couches,
benches or dirt.
Your friends, all dead.
You have to stop now
or you'll be dead too.

Come in,
make appointment.
Maybe you keep it.
Maybe you don't.

Tell Me About Despair

Tell me about despair, yours, and I will tell you mine ... — Mary Oliver, *Wild Geese*

I
I will give you a room
for your anger,
large enough to let it rip,
to let each blast

Bulge out the walls
the ceiling and the floor,
rock the room from side to side
and yet not tip.

When your rage has spent itself
let it lie, let it curl up
in a corner and sleep
until you waken it again.

II
I will give you a sack
for your resentments.
Pick them off your skin
like fleas, like lice, like maggots

Engorged with your heart's blood,
feeding and breeding in your wounds
so they ooze and putrefy
and never heal.

Toss each grub into the bag.
Tie it tight, stamp it flat.
Squeeze out every juicy drop of bile
and feed it to the flames.

III
I will give you a jar
For your worries.
When you are feeling fretful
hold it to your lips,

Pour in all your racing thoughts,
your sweaty palms,
your fluttery heart,
your churning gut,

All your misgivings,
past, present and to come.
Then, quick, screw on the lid.
When you are feeling bored

And restless, empty and alone,
take it out, shake it up.
Consider carefully,
what one sip would do.

IV
I will give you a box
for your sorrow,
rectangular,
long for your grief,

Deep for your despair,
narrow for your loneliness.
Set it on the kitchen shelf.
When you are sad

Take it down,
lift up the lid.
Out of it will rise
one endless wail

Like the long low note
of a lonesome train
throbbing through the midnight
deserts of your heart.

Sit at the table, listen
as it fills the air, watch
as it curls like smoke,
up and out and through

the darkened pane
to fill the empty spaces
between stars.
When you are done grieving,

Snap it shut.
Put it back
up on the shelf
until the next time.

✦

True North

Men at the jail
come in three varieties:
lost boys,
cool dudes,
old wrecks.

The lost boys
have just awoken
from their trance
of heroin or coke,
alcohol or oxys.

Their hair is tousled
or sticks straight up.
They can't quite catch on
to why they're here
or what they've done.

They want to know
how long they've got,
so they can get their shit together,
straighten out, before they're gone
at twenty-eight or thirty.

And each time they come back
I tell them, they're fine,
their liver will recover
if only they'll stop
drinking, drugging, dying.

The cool dudes
range from twenty-five to forty,
blue eyes, white teeth,
well-groomed, well-muscled,
even charming.

Backs straight,
chests out,
they swagger,
kings of pod 2B.
They've always got an angle.

The wrecks
slouch into medical
leading with their paunch.
They have diabetes, heart disease,
cirrhosis and ascites.

Off the juice
they're sad or angry
or encephalopathic,
truly believing this time
they'll be ready for rehab and a job.

The lost boys don't see,
and the cool dudes don't believe,
that the path from boy to dude to wreck
proceeds relentless,
unswerving,

True as a magnet to the pole
in one unbroken line.

Original version published in *The Permanente Journal* 2008 Fall; 12(4)

On the Pod

The door clangs shut.
The nurse and I walk in.
All eyes turn toward the diversion.
Two little female sticks
bobbing in a sea of men.

The room is large, and small,
swarming with elbows, feet, faces,
a buzzing hive of orange scrubs,
talking, joking, shoving,
pushing, pacing, roaming.

The ceiling is high, and low,
from two tiers up it presses down,
filled with a gray-brown cloud,
something nameless, edgy, hostile
and immeasurably sad.

I feel the stares of men looking,
and not looking at me,
wanting contact, conversation,
attention, sympathy,
distraction, wanting

Anything, anything at all.
I feel it pressing in on me
like thumbprints, collapsing me.
I shut down all my doors and windows,
and focus on a spot across the room

Where a thin bar of sunlight filters
through barbed wire to light a concrete court.

✦

Original version published in *The Permanente Journal* 2008 Fall; 12(4)

A Black Satin Ribbon

I'm on my way out late for a meeting.
The CNA stops me, says, "Take a look,"
and lifts Zoë's hair.

A glossy black line runs under her chin
from the tip of her right ear
to the tip of her left.
It glistens black with dried blood,
bristles blue with the sharp ends
of twenty-eight stitches that wave
like the legs of a blue nylon centipede
stuck upside-down
in the moist crust of her wound.

I went to 7-11, got a 6-pack and a razor.
Then I went to the park and drank the beer.
They brought me to the ER.
I was blue-papered.

"How long did they keep you?"
Overnight.
Then they arrested me,
for drunk and disorderly.

"Are you suicidal now?"
"No? Good."

I'm on my way out, late for a meeting.

The Lost Girls

I

Dora is gone, I know not where.
She sits on the edge of the table, talks to me,
but she's not there.

Her face is flat and round
a saucer with ears and curly hair.
Her fingers flit like grasshoppers
across her orange scrubs
as she recites her litany:
depression and anxiety
bipolar, PTSD,
paranoia, ADHD,
heroin, crack, and weed
oxys, vics and percs,
xanax, valium, twisted tea,
and cigarettes, 3 packs a day.

II

Loretta's missing too.
Dressed in a long green quilt,
holes for arms and neck.
Always suicidal,
always guarded one on one.
Drugged, heavy lids, slurred speech,
slow motion, still, she manages,
day after day, in the dark cave of her quilt,
to rip open a ten-inch wound
in her right thigh, deep and wide,
filleted, like an anatomy section,
displaying muscle, bone and tendon.

I check her wound for signs of infection.
I look in her eyes to see who's there
savaging her flesh, making the guards,
the nurses, the sheriff dance to her tune,
but she's long gone.

III

Ella has a face full of freckles,
thick, rich chestnut hair.
Her eyes, a deep sea blue,

Come back to me from far away
to give a yes or no, then drift again
to some point distant in time or space.

Some time before. Before
she stepped away to shoot a gram
and her infant drowned in his bath.

Some place besides Max, where she paces
the small rectangle of her cell and sees a guard
three times a day to give or take a tray.

Max, where she was put to keep her safe,
to keep her from being pecked to death
by all the other women on the pod.

The pod, where no one asks, no one tells,
but everyone knows, and every crime is rated
and Ella's is the lowest of the low,

Making her fit object for all simmering
frustrations, stifled outrage
and any random meanness

From women who have abandoned
scores of infants down the years
to the dubious mercies of foster care,

Women, who, given any opening,
would destroy her if they could
to prove their finer maternal feelings,

to redeem their losses, assuage their
    own guilt,
some crooked catharsis for the justice that
    has always eluded them.

✦

The reviewed studies show that from 55 percent to 99 percent of these women reported a history of physical or sexual trauma. Most of the trauma occurred before age 18 and was commonly related to repetitive childhood physical or sexual assault. "Exploring the Role of Child Abuse in Later Drug Abuse," NIDA (www.drugabuse.gov).

Even the Screws

Even the most jaded, hard-nosed, brown shirts,
crew cut, paunch and jowls,

The ones with no color vision, only black and white
in law, in life, in people,

Always bring them by medical on the way back
from sentencing

To ask me for an order, a valium, a klonopin, a sleeper,
because they know.

They know how the glacial cool off cinder blocks
seeps into your bones,

How the glare and buzz of white fluorescence
exposes every edge and flaw,

How the clang of metal doors, slammed one after another,
echoes and re-echoes

Through the raw chambers of your heart,
the dark tunnels of your mind,

And they know what it's like to leave at 4 p.m.

Cody

Just blew in from OK City,
got his diagnosis and came back to Maine
to be near family in his final days.
What, with the leukemia and all,
he didn't reckon they wouldn't want to be with him.
But, sure enough,
They wuz still mean as badgers.
They said, "Nice ta seeya," and changed the locks.
After that what else could he do?

He was only buying hisself a little pain relief,
a little comfort in a fifth of Jack.
But he only had a twenty,
forgot all about the tax.
They coulda skipped it.
So he just walked right on through
them sliding glass doors with it anyway.

Ma'am evra bone in my body aches
I uster ride the rodeo. I hadta quit.
I got busted so many times I couldn' ride no more.

I order morphine.

"Any allergies?"

 Possum.

"Possum?"

Have you never et possum Ma'am?
It is nastee!
✦

Carmen

Twenty-five.
Infection in her heart.
Blood clots in her lungs.
Open heart surgery.
Two strokes.
On blood thinners.
Still upright, no deficits.

Works as an escort.
Busted on Friday.

My mom doesn't get it.
She thinks I can just quit.
I made $900 this weekend.
Do you know how much heroin I can buy with that?

My dad'll make my bail.
He pays for my apartment,
buys me food and clothes.

The doctors said if I don't quit I'll die.
They say everything that's happened is because of heroin.
I don't get it.
Do you know why I have clots?

If only I could get her mind and body in the same room
together.

Circles of Hell

Sometimes, you don't know, you just walk in.
The door clangs shut behind you, it's too late to turn around.

It's a short walk from medical to max. My badge gets me through
the first door. Then I stand and wait for guards who sit all day
watching banks of cctvs, to see and buzz me through the second.
Then I wait for the cctv guards to tell the guards in max I'm there.
They let me in when they feel like it.

Sixteen single cells, eight to a tier, four to a block,
reinforced steel, plexiglass, concrete
a small cinderblock lobby,
TV always on, a few worn paperback Bibles.
Each block has a small corridor with a metal table
and two metal benches bolted to the floor.
Each cell door has a flap at the bottom
where food get passed.

Only time I was ever scared
was sitting at one of those little tables,
inmate on the other side, shackled hands and ankles,
guard behind him shooting the shit
with two other guards in the lobby.
The man was telling me he had both a vagina *and* testicles.
He wanted me to verify it. That was ok,
I said I could do that.

But then he started to rumble,
just a little at first, then shake all over
like a volcano about to erupt,
like a fault line about to fracture,
and swallow me, him, the table.
Even shackled, this guy could do some damage
before they had the wits to pull him off.
I got up, ever so slowly, and slipped away.

But, I still didn't know,
know it was hell,
not then,
not till later.

Sitting at a little metal table again,
waiting for a prisoner, a tiny voice wafts up to me.
I look around trying to find it,
but it's coming from the floor,
like a mouse squeaking from its hole.

Hey, doc. Docta Dowd, it's me, Lenny, remember me?
Remember that stuff you gave me for my face,
the pills, the cream? It works, my face looks good,
real good, thanks, Doc,
thanks a lot.

He must have been lying like a snake on his belly
on the cold stone floor of his cell, one arm propping
the food flap open, his neck twisted round,
his mouth to the hole

To tell me something, anything,
a little chitchat,
a little give and take,
before the guard comes by
and boots it shut.

Ambien: a commom prescription sleeping pill.

Ascites: excess fluid build-up in the abdomen from liver disease.

BAL: blood alcohol level.

Blue-papered: involuntary commitment to the hospital.

Boot: to inject.

Forties: 40-ounce bottles of high alcohol content beer.

Hang a sign or fly a sign: stand by the roadside with a cardboard sign asking for money.

High gravity: beer that has higher alcohol content by percent.

Jonesing: slang for withdrawing.

Max: maximum-security cell block.

Narcan: naloxone, an opioid blocker that is used to reverse opioid overdoses. Firemen, police, and rescue workers carry it. It can be given as a shot in a large muscle or as a nasal spray. Now patients and family members can have it by prescription in many states. It may be carried over the counter in pharmacies soon. It is being used so often it has become a verb.

Natty Daddies: 25-ounce cans of 8% beer, very cheap.

Oxys: oxycodone.

Percs: percoset.

Suboxone: a medication that treats craving for opiates. It is a combination of buprenorphine, an opioid, and naloxone, an opioid blocker. The blocker is added to deter IV use. Suboxone works wonderfully well for opioid cravings and helps many, many patients get their lives back. But, it is often diverted, that is, sold or shared by patients who have a prescription for it. The people who buy it on the street are mostly treating their opiate addiction and withdrawal symptoms. The people who sell it are making money. It has a high street value, $20 to $25/dose in Maine.

Subutex: buprenorphine without the naloxone component. It is used in pregnancy.

Vics: Vicodin.

Wellbutrin: an antidepressant that some people inject to get high.

Xannies: Xanax, a commonly abused benzodiazepine.

Major risk factors for developing addiction are childhood traumas: abuse, neglect or loss. Most of my patients' childhoods were full of chaos or violence. Neglect was the best they could hope for.

About the Author

Mary Dowd, MD, is a physician specializing in addiction in the homeless population in Portland, ME. She works in detox, at various addiction clinics, and sometimes does a stint at the county jail. She is married and has four grown children. Her poems have appeared in various journals and in the Hippocrates Prize Anthology 2017. She has led poetry workshops for the Transformational Language Arts Network at Goddard College in Plainfield, VT, and The Examined Life Conference in Iowa City, IA. For many years she led a workshop reading and writing poetry with men in long-term treatment for addiction at Milestone Foundation.